MW00357026

Dreamscapes

by
Ethan Goffman

UnCollected Press

Dreamscapes
Copyright © 2021 by Ethan Goffman

All rights reserved. This book in full form may not be used or reproduced by electronic or mechanical means without permission in writing from the author and UnCollected Press.

Cover Art:
Journey to Incarnation
Henry G. Stanton
24"x20" acrylic gouache on canvas
www.brightportfal.com

Back Cover Photo: Amy Goffman

Book Design by:

UnCollected Press
8320 Main Street, 2nd Floor
Ellicott City, MD 21043

For more books by UnCollected Press:
www.therawartreview.com

First Edition 2021
ISBN: 978-1-7378731-1-2

To Marianne, Thelma, and Callie.

Special Thanks to Marianne Szlyk, Will Mayo, and Mark Keats for reading and commenting upon the manuscript. Additional thanks to Alan Britt, Jerry Eisner, and Dr. Michael Anthony Ingram for their enthusiastic support.

Table of Contents

Preface

Are these dreams or are they reality? That's an easy question. And yet reality is at least as impalpable as dreams (and may only exist as a kind of illusion). The animals we eat, the jobs we toil at, the machines we use (and that use us), the complex combinations of sound and texture emanating from our mouths, the floating shapes we gaze at upon computer screens, are stranger than any dream. They have become normal to us in the way, say, a prison guard's work seems normal in the daily routine as prisoners are counted, strip searched, marched around, and made less than human in myriad ways.

Ephemera

The future exists in an enormous stack of folded paper. The goddess of time, with a smooth, innocent face ancient before its time, gently yanks pages from the stack bit by bit and flings them ruthlessly, with great love, in front of humanity, where events pop up in bounteous, multi-dimensional color. That is how time unfolds. Before a page is unfolded, it is the future; the instant we see it, it becomes the past. We only view time in terms of the present, but the present does not exist. In a way, we do not exist.

Family Life

I was frantically trying to call my father, sometimes several times a day, but I could never get through. A voice would announce that no one was there to take my call, or that the number was no longer in service, or I would just experience an interminable beeping, or occasionally a person would answer, not quite male or female, speaking a strange language with clicks and grunts not quite human, or I would get a voicemail and leave a message that was never answered, or I would get nothing at all. I had no idea why I wanted to reach my father so badly, or even if he was still alive. One day I realized that the number I had been calling so frantically these many years was my own.

In the Beginning

I haven't been myself since a horrible, traumatic event overturned my life.

Birth.

Nirvana in a Pill

The little man with the sweetness of Nirvana written in the creases on his face had given me the pill I'd long prayed for. It was the pill with the answer to life, happiness, why we are here, why there is evil, whether there is an afterlife, and the meaning of it all. I swallowed it down with a shot of whisky, as he had instructed, and began the 24-hour wait for it to take effect.

That night, a resonant voiceover interrupted my dreams to warn of unintended side effects. "Caution—this pill may cause blurred vision, dizziness, tortured breathing, suicidal thoughts, paranoia, diarrhea, constipation, hallucinations, palpitations, sheer frustration, indignation, anger all around the nation, strange visions, delusions of grandeur, feelings of utter despair and insignificance, nightmares, daymares, I-just-don't-caremares, myopia, dystopia, give-up-hopia. If you experience any or all of these, do not call your doctor—it is too late!"

As I awoke, the strange little man's face appeared floating in the air like a balloon. "Perhaps I should have explained that the 24-hour period for this pill to take effect is a metaphor," he said. "The actual waiting period is an entire lifetime, from dawn to dusk of the body and soul."

Youth Lives on Within Us

I am in my old, boyhood home, in my small room, in quarantine due to the pandemic. Across the hall, in the enormous master bedroom, my parents lie passive in their bed, speaking a few occasional words, asking, for instance, if I'm hungry and, if I say yes, suggesting "then go get yourself some food." In the basement apartment dwells my wife. We have, after all, plenty of space, so why shouldn't we each have our own room? However, my room is by far the smallest, barely big enough to stretch out. My wife does come upstairs to brighten up my day, although she has trouble ascending the endless, twisting staircase that doubles and triples back upon itself, to reach my solitary room. Is my sister living somewhere in the house, perhaps a hidden or forgotten room? No, she moved away eons ago, to Mexico, I think, where she has become some sort of minor goddess to those who still follow the old ways from before Columbus. I don't believe they rip out the bleeding, beating heart of a virgin in homage to my sister, but who knows for sure? I don't hear from her more than once every eon or so, and even that may be a dream. It is time-consuming for her, being a goddess, even a minor one ministering to the remnants of a broken people.

We Drink in the Universe in a Cup of Tea

One day the universe shrank to a trillionth its previous size. Meanwhile, time itself sped up by a factor of a trillion. Here on Earth, nobody noticed, as everything was proportionately the same. Every morning, we drank our unfathomably miniscule cups of coffee and ate our nano eggs and toast, believing they were as large as ever. We drove our infinitesimal cars to office buildings so small as to barely exist, believing they were as massive and comforting and solid as before. We were as bored as ever at our grinding work, not realizing it was completed virtually at the instant we began. At night, we gazed up at the heavens, at stars strewn like salt, turmeric, and cayenne pepper across the globe of the sky, now small enough to fit into a cup of tea. We did not realize how insignificant we had all become.

My Heroic Life

Outlaws had captured me, stolen my gold, tied me to a stake, doused me with gasoline, and were ready to set me aflame, when who should swoop in to save me but the Lone Ranger and Tonto. Tonto untied me with firm, gentle hands, but gazed down shyly when I looked at him. As the outlaws scattered to the four winds like evil dandelion seeds, I noticed that the Lone Ranger was wearing a mask over his nostrils and mouth rather than the customary mask over the upper part of his face.

Later that night, Tonto convulsed with coronavirus fever and died first thing in the morning. "No worries," said the Lone Ranger. "It always happens with Injun sidekicks—it's their fate. I'll just gallop on down to the reservation and find me a new one." What about me? I thought. Will I die of coronavirus? Or will my white skin save me?

As the Lone Ranger galloped off, I noticed that his horse also had a coronavirus mask. A ferocious looking desert bee stung me and even it was wearing a coronavirus mask, or so it seemed to me, although the attack was swift, and the creature buzzed about so it was hard to tell for certain.

A few days later, having survived a mysterious fever, chills, heat, shivering shaking quivering, headaches splitting my skull, numbness of legs and feet, hallucinations, a brief encounter with Satan, a briefer encounter with the divine, I headed to the latest superhero convention, although with real superheroes, not the fakes dressed up in silly costumes you usually find at such affairs. Even the superheroes had ceased wearing full face masks, though, and had donned an array of ornate, exotic, and colorful coronavirus masks. They did practice social distancing.

Back Home in Indiana

Once again, I was returning to my ancestral home in Indiana where over a thousand generations of Goffmans had lived, bored out of our minds and wondering how we had ended up stuck in this god-forsaken land of small towns, racists, cornfields, and cow tipping. I felt a strong urge to return to my roots, in the soil and blood of a university town, and stood in line at the bus depot. It was easy to buy a ticket to Indianapolis, the only town in Indiana that was actually on the map. But, since the rest of the state is uncharted territory, how would I ever find my ancestral homeland? Did a bus even go there? And did my hometown have a name? I couldn't quite remember. Plus, the last Goffman had pulled up roots and emigrated when my sister moved to Texas well over a century ago. I had no home, was as rootless as a cob of corn plucked from the Hoosier soil and shipped by airplane to a shining supermarket in a distant country.

Our Place in the Universe

It is possible we're the only planet in the universe on which advanced life forms evolved. It is possible we're just one of billions of worlds teeming with life. Some scientists attempted to come up with a formula evaluating the possibility of life on other worlds by assigning a probability to different aspects, such as water and a moderate temperature, but the truth is, no one knows. It would be like trying to evaluate the number of cakes in different houses by figuring out the probability that they have all the different ingredients—flour, sugar, butter, leavening, etc. But will the ingredients spontaneously form into a cake or do they need a chef?

Creationists could use this analogy to argue for the existence of God, the divine chef so to speak, but who cares. True believers are arrogant and foolish in their own special way, just as militant atheists are arrogant and foolish in their way. The only philosophy that makes any sense is utter uncertainty. Or perhaps I am being arrogant and foolish in making this pronouncement.

Old Age

"Help me, help me!" said my father in a piteous, whining voice, yet also strangely sonorous, over and over and over. "What should I do?" I asked. "What should I do?" "Nobody can help me. Nobody can help me."

The Future Is Predictable, It's the Past that's a Mystery

A week from today, I will be interviewing a futurist about the year 2563 for an online magazine. Unlike most futurists, this one actually foresees the future, with a 100% success rate. She has transcended time and space, sees, hears, smells, feels, and knows all. In the year 2563, she will tell me, the human race will be long gone, the animals we know mostly vanished; no squirrels scampering, no horses galloping, no sloths lollygagging from trees. The Earth will be battered by climate change and by two small nuclear wars, between Israel and Iran and between India and Pakistan. As an exclamation point, the hand of god—or a random gesture from the emptiness of the cosmos—will send a massive asteroid to pummel our planet. This will not be the end, as life is clever and adaptive and new species will even then begin to arise. It will be the culmination of one *Maha Yuga,* one Great Age. Everything will be utterly transformed. Everything will be the same.

Profound, Yet Useless, Advice

The most cynical man in the world spoke to me. "Just remember," he said, "pain and suffering last forever. Joy is fleeting."

Dreamscapes

In my dream, everything is different. Time is linear and people are rational. I am a writer living in a vast white marble house in which skylights shine white light on my gleaming white Mac. I type diligently, composing troubled dreamscapes while waiting for my wife to arrive home in her bright white power suit. I think she is a medical doctor, or perhaps director of a development agency, someone powerful who helps large numbers of people, someone far more accomplished than I. Each day takes place exactly as the last. Every year winter comes, but the snow quickly melts away. Each summer swells with azaleas and begonias that soon shed, littering the ground with snow white and blood red.

Every day I write out my dreams, although I have mostly forgotten them and must invent abundantly. Or perhaps I only think I have forgotten and every detail is exactly as they occurred in my dreams. Or perhaps I never dream and never sleep but have spent all of eternity composing imaginary dreams on this gleaming computer, like, as Marianne Moore said, imaginary gardens with real toads.

The Biosphere

In the late morning, with sun streaming and heat wave pounding, two racoons amble across a grassy field, not sneaky thieves but mischievous kids. I sneak close to glimpse their tiny masked faces. The raccoons are not graceful, but stumble forward. They are built according to the same plan as all mammals, two eyes, a nose, a mouth, four limbs: symmetry, to take in what the good Earth has to offer. But why are they rambling through the day when raccoons are furtive night creatures? Are they relocating due to the extreme heat, or perhaps a nearby construction project? God speed and help the racoons, two tiny creatures in a world made cruel.

Youth

When I was 19, I played bass, very badly, for a punk rock band called Covid 19. But wait, you say, that was way before the disease ever existed. Curious, I tried to contact, over Facebook, the group's members (or at least the surviving ones—one is dead, three of us remain). I asked Chris how she could have come up with that name (Chris was a he at the time, but that's a different story). She said, as far as she remembered, it just sounded cool. But then she wasn't sure—perhaps Oliver, who had been killed in a car accident some 20 years ago, had come up with the name. Chris had, in fact, contracted Covid 19 (the disease, not the punk rock group) and been in a state of fevered delirium, but had survived. Perhaps this whole thing is a dream in Chris's fevered imagination and there never was such a band. Meanwhile, the fourth and final member of the band, who had played electronic keyboards that sang like drunken, furious gods, has not spoken to us in years, has not answered my "friend" request. He is, in fact, a part of a hugely successful Rock band.

You're Gonna Make It on Your Own

Then there was the guy who ran into Mary Tyler Moore in person and said, "Oh, you're still alive." Perhaps he added, "I thought you had died long, long, long ago." Or perhaps he didn't say that at all. Perhaps he said, surprised, "I thought you were just a character on TV? You're a real person." Perhaps he was, himself, just a character on TV who ran into the older Mary Tyler Moore playing herself as a real person, but it was all an act. Perhaps Laura Petrie, the wife on the old Dick van Dyke show, later became an actress and took on the role of Mary Tyler Moore, a fictional actress who had played the real Laura Petrie on TV.

Strange Things Happen in Our Wonderful Home

Somehow, a large gourd filled with crickets appeared in our kitchen. A few had escaped and were traipsing about the house, happy and free. Or were they bewildered and on the verge of panic? In any case, I would have to open the gourd to free the rest using our oversized kitchen knife, which no longer cut like it used to. Slicing the end off the gourd, I cut my finger and a large drop of blood landed with a splash on the ground. As the crickets tumbled out, I rushed to open the door to the outside and the thick mass of crickets sprung out and scattered on the lawn to face the fall chill. I shook the gourd and a few small bodies tumbled to the ground.

The day that preceded this dream, a huge spider, half spooky half friendly, was trapped in our kitchen sink. Using some aging Tupperware, I was able to rescue it and put it outside. Later that day, as I was cooking, a cricket was trapped in the very same sink. "Oh, good grief," I said, exasperated, and used a paper towel to crush it, then put its broken little body into the trash.

The Pure Soul

One fine day, I ran into a person who was all soul, no body. You might think this was in a dream, but it was on an ordinary street on a sunny weekend morning.

"How did you do it?" I asked the pure soul. "How did you achieve life without a body?"

"You are asking the wrong questions."

"Did you ever have a body? Did you achieve Nirvana? Or are you just as confused and contradictory, as driven by selfishness but also, at times, empathy, as any other human?"

"You are asking the wrong questions."

"All right. Should we just try to have a normal conversation?"

The pure soul did not answer.

"Beautiful weather today," I said, trying to be friendly, but with the ulterior motive of getting the pure soul to talk, bit by bit to reveal the mysteries of the universe.

"It is a lovely day," said the pure soul, "although, for me, no lovelier than any other day."

"I've been fully vaccinated," I said. "So there's no chance I'll spread the coronavirus. Although, I suppose for you that doesn't matter."

The pure soul did not answer.

"Can you get, like, mystical viruses? Like, in the same way that computer viruses spread, are their viruses that exist on a spiritual plain?"

"Hey," said a young dude with a wisp of a goatee who happened to be passing by. "You're talking to yourself. Are you on wireless?"

"You wouldn't understand," I said. "You are too young, too caught up in technology and the physical world."

"All right dude, just asking." With that he was gone and the pure soul, too, had vanished.

I walked on into the gentle sunshine, the mild wind caressing me, my chance of learning the mysteries of the universe disappeared.

Mystery Solved!

In a flash, I had it. THE ANSWER! To life, the universe, and everything. And it wasn't 42, but something far more profound and beautiful, the actual, singular answer in a form that one could write down beautifully and instantly. I grabbed a pen and notepad to scribble it down, but alas the pen was out of ink. I grabbed a second pen, but that, too was empty. Desperately, I searched the room for another, combed every crack and cranny. I was down on my knees among piles of paper, an archive of my entire existence prior to the Internet. The sea of papers rose up, covered my crouching body. Why hadn't I thrown this mess away? A clean house is an efficient house.

Damn—never a pen when you need one! I remembered a pleasant new Bic, swelling with ink, that had fallen out of my pocket in the yard the other evening when it was too dark to see, so I scurried outside to search for it. But the garden had some sorry looking weeds that needed plucking, so I had to take care of that. I felt pity for the scrawny, pathetic looking plants that were only a minor nuisance to the flowers and bushes I desired, but still I pulled them up forcefully by the roots. And look, under a nearby bush! A pen!

When I returned indoors, I had, of course, utterly forgotten the answer to life, the universe, and everything. But I realized that I needed to add toothpaste to my grocery list. Maybe that was the answer. Just do one damn thing after another till eventually you die.

I need to add pens to the grocery list.

The Cynic

I've known that Santa Claus didn't exist since I was a baby. I was a born cynic. Hell, I even knew that Tibet didn't exist, or Shangri La, or Timbuktu, these lost lands of legend. And I certainly knew that UFOs had never visited the Earth, that the Loch Ness monster, Tyrannosaurus Rex, and pygmies were all stories told to frighten little children.

An Intruder

A woman and her adolescent son had barged into my home uninvited, claiming they were long-lost relatives. While the woman went back out to her car to "take care of some things," I asked the son, who had curly red hair that matched his acne, in what way our families were related. He wasn't sure, but thought it was through Weak Doug, his grandfather. I didn't recall a Doug in our branch of the family, but we had argued with many cousins. What was left was a small, isolated branch, and since an unknown number of relatives had been eliminated by the Nazis back in the old world, there weren't many left. Perhaps it was best to take whatever relatives we could.

At that moment, the woman returned with two huge suitcases that dwarfed her slight frame. "Are you planning on staying with us?" I asked.

"We have nowhere else to go," she told me. "But we can cook and clean and we're very quiet."

Not having a car, I thought she could also be useful for running errands. But what would my wife say?

"I'll replace your wife," said the woman, reading my thoughts. "I may not look it, but I'm a tiger in bed." A flush of arousal surged through me, but also embarrassment that she had said this in front of her 13 year old son.

"It's no problem, I know the ways of the world," murmured the son as he huddled in the corner, his face so scarlet that his pimples seemed about to burst, his curly orange hair poised to spring from his head.

Making a Spectacle of My Life

In the darkest dark of night, reaching for a Kleenex on the bedstand, I knocked over my glasses. I reached below to find a vast pile of aging glasses that I had kept stored there, from my years of malfunctioning vision. Well, I thought, I'll get the correct pair in the morning, and tumbled into a violent sleep with hallucinogenic dreams, not quite nightmares.

Awoken by a trickle of light sneaking through the window, I peered below, with fuzzy, disoriented vision, and grabbed at a multitude of glasses, a spectacle of spectacles. Glasses were piled to the ceiling and, for me to even arise from bed, would need to be removed. I had no idea that I'd gone through that many spectacles. I must have lived for eons.

The first pair I grabbed was for extreme farsightedness. It had allowed me to read deeply into tiny typeface, to discern things unimaginable to the average person. These glasses had been useful back in the day, but they had also confused me, making it impossible to proceed with the serious business of life. The second pair, for near-sightedness, had allowed me to view distant stars, nebulae, and galaxies, and to at least begin to understand such mysteries as dark matter and alternative universes. I remembered that, with these glasses, I'd seen the edge of the universe at one point, but not quite beyond—but I realized that they would eventually drive me insane, and so abandoned them. The third pair allowed me to look through things. Yes, I could view naked women, and they had no idea, but also naked men, as well as a variety of aging bodies, which had their own beauty but also disgust. This pair of glasses had felt more and more intrusive and even horrible and, after a few short years, I had given them up (actually, I had vowed to do so immediately, but somehow day followed day, rather as if one had a huge box of slightly stale jelly donuts and couldn't stop eating). The fourth pair allowed me to peer into people's thoughts, which was far more horrible than examining their bodies, and these had barely lasted a moment. The fifth pair revealed the horrors of history—which made me despise the human spirit—but also the course of evolution—which left me in awe at the wonders of nature—all the way back to the Big Bang, or at least the instant after. With this pair of glasses, I had learned that science, Genesis, and the vast variety of human myths and religions do not contradict each other, although they don't quite reveal truth, either. The sixth pair showed the end of humanity, revealing what a marvelous species we are, and into the future far beyond, where cockroaches had evolved to replace us and fulfill the grand promise we only thought we had. The seventh pair revealed ultimate meaning, but they burned my hands, so I was unable to put them on. Alas, I could not find, amid the vast and ever-growing pile, my current pair of glasses which made me, for once in my life, a normal human being. So now I hobble about, virtually blind.

A Message from Beyond

I was with Perry, a jovial man with mildly crinkly skin. We were on the street of some city and he was speaking of mysteries and riddles with a shop keeper. His many puns, while not funny, revealed multitudes about the cosmic order. At least I thought they did—the exact words have slipped like pancakes off the griddle of memory.

Perry had been recovering from heart surgery. And now COVID 19 was complicating all medical care, putting everyone at risk. I wondered whether he had died and was contacting me from the next world, letting me know that everything is gloriously profound and humorous, in a trivial sort of way.

Writing the World in Ghostly Shadows

I am writing these dreams on my industrial-strength home computer, the world's largest computer, larger even than those enormous computers back in the mid twentieth century, when I was small and snuck into the Great computer building at Purdue University, where my father taught. There, I saw the vast machine that covered a whole room, if not many rooms, a vast maze, for computers then took up more space than a football field yet had less power than a tiny device today you keep on a ring on your pinkie finger. But now, in the far future, I need a computer the size of Trenton, New Jersey to contain all that I wish to write about. I am ambitious, want to discuss the vast scope of humanity, the sun and stars, the galaxies, and our tiny part within it all, the multiverse themselves, oh who am I kidding, I'll be lucky to add an infinitesimal fragment to the human endeavor known as literature, meant to capture the most profound emotions, dreams, and thoughts. Did I write all this or did I dream it or only dream that I wrote it or write that I dreamt it or dream that I wrote that I dreamt? This is tedious and has already gone on far too long, yet could potentially continue forever, $n + 1$ in an endless loop.

The Creation

In a bout of insomnia, I decided I would pass the time by dreaming the world into existence. I began by separating the light from the air, the air from the water, the water from the firm soil. Using clippings from my fingernails, flakes from my drying skin, hairs from under my arms, sweat, a bit of saliva, and a few drops of blood, I filled the world with flora and fauna, with plankton and shrimp and darting fishies in the oceans, with gnarly vines and looping trees, creeping creatures with multiple legs and eye sockets on the land, fluttering butterflies and birds on outspread wings soaring through the vast air.

"Wait a second," I exclaimed in a booming voice that echoed through all time and space! "It's all been done before"! I decided to visit the actual God to voice my complaint. Ascending to the actual heaven, I bowed and trembled as I spoke. "It's all been done before," I said. "You've left me nothing new or original to create in the torpor of my puny human mind." My thoughts echoed and reached myself. They reverberated through the imaginary heavens in my mind and the churning, anxious hell of my soul.

i imagined faintly i heard god's answer. "i was bored, too," she said.

The Power of Yoga

You know you've had a cosmic, mind-blowing experience when you've lost all track of time. Once, ten thousand years had passed and I didn't even know it. I had returned to existence as a new being. Now, however, I can't begin to concentrate on yoga, can't even conceive of being "in the moment," as a million thoughts, anxieties, worries, duties, itches, twitches, pointless desires scratch at the tender flesh of my soul, drawing blood, while I strain to contort my body into pretzel shapes, or even fail at the child's pose. So I have given up yoga or any form of meditation. Is it possible that I had, many many millennia ago, achieved oneness with the universe and have now thrown it all away?

Gimpel the Fooling Myself

In an eerie dream, my wife confessed her many past affairs, crying half the time, laughing half the time. Her tears formed a rapidly rising ocean of salty water that stung my flesh and flooded my nostrils. I awoke within the dream, and, when I confronted my wife, she told me she had contemplated affairs but never actually had one. What could I say? I am the same.

In real life, I don't ask my wife this paranoid question. I follow Gimpel the Fool, the Isaac Bashevis Singer character who, although it seemed likely that his wife's children were from other men, pretended never to doubt her. Indeed, he raised these children as his own. In this way, Gimpel had as decent a life as possible in this broken world of lies and condescension.

The Many Ages of Man

Sometimes I feel like I've failed at being an adult. I wasn't much good at being a child, either. And don't even mention adolescence!

Perspective

"Why are you so miserable? You're an old man with a bright future behind you. Also a wretched, depressing future, but what can you expect from life? We all go through, or will go through, or remember our young selves as they contemplate going through a future where they will, at some point, face: rejection, boredom, suffering. And the final act? Death. But that is overshadowed, in our young selves, by the bright and shiny hope of greatness."

A Short Trip

I was taking a massive industrial elevator, swelling with passengers who seemed friendly enough but mostly kept to themselves. I was going home, to apartment 523! (In real life, which is also a dream, our small house is at 523 N Muffet St.) The elevator reached the correct floor, and I stood a disturbingly long time waiting for the doors to open, perhaps the time it took for the origin of the universe, which is both nothing and all of infinity. Instead, the contraption I was in, not quite an elevator but more like a bus, took off through the neighborhood, wandering past the cold doors of various apartments, meandering through the fringes of the suburbs, past tiny houses with withered, broken shutters. I returned to my seat on the elevator/bus, glancing at the other passengers' blank white faces (even the faces of the black people were somehow pale white). I slumped in my seat, wondering when, oh when, I would ever be home again and indeed if I ever had had a home, if my whole life had been a journey with no beginning and no end, if I had, perhaps in some other dream, had a real home where I could feel at peace, where happiness and light shone.

Explanatory Interlude

In a time when not just every family has a car, but every member of every family, even the cats and dogs, readers may be confused—but yes, it's true, not only do I survive without a car, but so does my wife. Our cats, Callie and Thelma, don't even have driver's licenses (they opted out due to environmental concerns about the impact of driving).

Time and Again

Like a good piece of music, the joyful interludes, little terrors and humiliations that visit one nightly develop the same themes but with infinite changes, some subtle, some roaring at you like a beast in a horror movie. In one, an old friend was coming to our apartment to help us move, but he was late. Meanwhile, my wife was missing, and I was supposed to pack for a move to a city so distant I wasn't sure whether they spoke English, or even walked upon two legs, but it was unclear what, of our many possessions, I was to keep and what to throw away and my wife would be infinitely angry if I made even the tiniest mistake. In another dream, I was to give a two-minute presentation on Jews in the Ottoman Empire, but that was my brother's expertise, and I knew nothing about it. But the timer had started, and I stood at the lectern and began this important presentation on an obscure and meaningless subject. I read from my notes, almost too tiny to see, a quotation that seemed to have nothing to do with the topic at hand. I figured I would fake my way through the meaning of the quotation, but somehow the notes had slipped from me. I had some other notes, large and sprawling, in my wife's handwriting, but I realized this was a grocery list.

Eek, a Mouse!

I had put out mouse traps a few weeks ago and almost forgot. Retrieving them so that Marianne, Thelma, and I didn't accidentally set them off, I found something unexpected. A dead mouse. When I had used traps a couple of years earlier, they had failed to catch anything, and I had resorted to poison.

As I dragged the trap from behind the refrigerator with a ruler, I thought I glimpsed a wadded-up piece of gray velvet that had gotten tangled up. But no. I examined its small face to ascertain that it was, indeed, a mouse, before throwing it away. That night, I dreamed that another mouse had appeared in the living room and I would have to set new traps.

Or perhaps I am just a dream in the mind of the mouse, a realization of its deepest terrors, out to destroy it for no reason whatsoever. Perhaps, to the mouse, I am proof that God does not exist, for how could a just and loving God create such an evil being?

In my dream—or the mouse's dream of what a creature such as me might dream—I also spot a tiny, furtive shape. A baby mouse? The next in a long line of my victims. Enmity between human and mouse is without end.

Sour Dreams

I was out with my wife—she had errands to run and then Catholic mass—when I remembered I had to be home at 10 AM sharp for an appointment that could change my life. But I realized I'd left my keys at home. I thought about asking my wife to cut her day short and come home, but instead found myself asking for the key. She fished it out of her pocket. As I gazed at her, something seemed strange and I realized it wasn't really her but another woman entirely. Why had she been trying to fool me? Or perhaps it was an innocent mistake?

Suddenly, I looked to my left and saw the soft features of my actual wife. She had been there all along. But now I had a strange silver key in my pocket, to what and where? My wife glared at me, as though I'd committed some unspeakable crime.

Riddle, Riddle

I was gazing up at crazy, glowing shapes for no reason with no rhyme. I would describe them, but they are beyond description, beyond imagination. I have amnesia over what they looked like— If I could remember, perhaps I'd have the secret to life itself. I gazed up at them, wondering if I would lie there, staring at these ineffable shapes, forever and beyond.

I awoke to find myself in a bathroom with the tub full, almost overflowing. I raced to the door, but it was locked. I tried the bolt—it was rigid for an instant, but then opened easily. I scurried through a series of bathrooms. At the end was a final bathroom in which stood three boys. "Why are you tormenting me," I asked. "Why won't you let me wake up"?

"You have us all wrong," said the oldest. "We don't even exist. We are the secret to life itself, if you only knew it. In fact you do, you know it profoundly, but your brain has no way to process the knowledge—which is not knowledge in any form that you understand it—even for an instant."

Lost

I was in a busy downtown. My wife and her friends were gossiping merrily, heading toward the next in a long series of poetry readings, but I was tired and told them I would rather go home. I waved goodbye and watched them dwindle in the distance. Then I remembered that we had recently moved and I wasn't sure where the new house was. It was a little yellow cottage and I thought the address was something like 535 Virgin Street. Even when we lived in the old house, I was never sure if I could find it, though I had somehow always managed. But this new one was in an even more obscure corner of the city and I imagined wandering around some dusky street as the sun set, spending the night on a park bench, perhaps being robbed or worse. I decided to chase down my wife, but she had already faded in the distance. My legs felt like lead as I slogged forward, struggling futilely, unable to run.

Cattle Farm

Without knowing why, I had somehow inherited a cattle farm in West Virginia. I found a peace I had never known herding the great creatures, so large and stoic and stupid and profound and sweet, among the sharp green fields and hills beneath a bright blue sky. They made soft thrumming noises as if speaking to me, or to the universe. Perhaps the universe answers them? It never answers me, but I am too neurotic and self-aware, so the universe is smart to ignore me.

I got to know individual cows. Elsa was my favorite, mainly snow white with patches of brown soft fur. She would rub her rough tongue against my hand. It seemed to be love. These massive beasts that could have easily trampled me were gentle as lambs.

I feel horrendous that I will have to sell them to be slaughtered. I might become vegetarian. The smell and bloodiness of meat has become disgusting. Still, I need to sell these cows off. That's the way the economics of a farm works. You always hurt the ones you love.

Another Lost Dream

I was on a subway, a bit late for an appointment. My tablet was telling me it was 8:22 so I had better hurry.

The train surfaced from the subterranean darkness into a blazing light. I checked my smart phone and it contradicted my tablet; it was only 8:14, so I had just enough time.

Exiting the subway, I glanced at the electronic clock that towered over the street. 9:25, I would be horribly late to this extremely important appointment. I would miss out on the opportunity that I desperately needed.

But wait a second. Perhaps that clock was wrong and my smart phone correct, in which case I would just make the meeting. I hurried along, only to realize I was on the wrong street. Or rather, on the correct street, Wisconsin Avenue, but in altogether the wrong city. I had taken the subway when, in fact, I should have taken Metrorail.

Overhead, a huge clock tower gave the time: 6:25. Indeed, the city was still dark and I would just have time to take Amtrak, then Uber, and, if I was lucky, make the appointment and proceed onward to a successful future. This was true even though I was an old man, a bit withered, and had already thrown away most of my life.

But wait a second. It wasn't dark at all—that had been a momentary rolling of gray clouds overhead, angry and ready to pounce like scampering rats. Now, indeed, the bright mid-day sun beat down.

But perhaps it was the wrong day entirely, or the wrong week, or even the wrong year. Indeed, the squat gray city looked as though it belonged to the wrong century—perhaps London in the industrial age—and I had decades, or even the whole of my life, to wait for the appointment.

I should have known there was a disruption in the timeline. In the real world, Trump could never have been elected president. I would be a famous author, recipient of a MacArthur genius grant, Pulitzer, or even the Nobel Prize, living in a gleaming mansion on a private hill at the edge of the city.

More likely, I would have been homeless at thirty and long ago dead on the street.

Support the Arts

I was an avant-garde artist on an interminable trip for my latest project—a recording of toilets flushing around the world. I imagined a meditative, ambient experience of whooshing, gurgling, gargling, burping, hiccupping, chirping, swooshing, sloshing, and innumerable other sounds—whatever the human mind can conjure and bring into existence for the crucial task of zipping our wastes rapidly away so that we never have to conceive of them again. I conceived this recording playing, not in museums or other mansions of fine arts, but roadside diners and fast food restaurants where people eating could imagine the final result of their consumption, part of the cycle of nature, and become one with the food experience, from corn and cows on abundant farms; to grim workers on production lines; to cooks and wait staff in harried kitchens; to one's taste buds dancing in a frenzy of pleasure, stimulated by plentiful fat, salt, and sugar; to the slow inner grumblings and acid workings of digestion; to the final glory of having one's wastes returned, not to enrich the soil, but into the sewers far away, travelers, perhaps, to some distant river or lake, or even into the deep ocean.

I had explained this grand conception when applying for grants for my project, but alas, the narrow minds that judge such things hadn't comprehended the brilliance of my vision and had rejected me at every turn. So I was using my own money for this journey, and when that ran out I planned to max out my credit cards. Finally, I would have to depend on the good will of those whom I met. Perhaps I would end up a beggar on some Calcutta street or dead while scaling a Himalayan peak? I wondered what kind of toilets they had up there, above and beyond the edge of the world. But that was the purpose of my journey, not to research the quality or aural properties of toilets around the world—which I could easily have found out on the internet—but to experience the grand variety of toilets myself. And now I was setting out on this artistic journey, to suffer and perhaps die along the way. But that's the point of art—not to produce some commercial product to display to the vapid public, but a voyage of discovery. Indeed, failure is the ultimate meaning of art, far more than success, which is a kind of selling out of the soul.

But O God how I yearned to be praised, to have my art move millions, to attain the status of a god!

Life Advice

Vacationing in a small hut on the beach, or rather attending an unimportant convention, we stepped outside to a glorious morning: blazing sun, sparkling sand, gulls glinting and squawking as they swooped above, ocean waves dancing upon the beach. We began the long walk to the convention hall, my wife impatiently ahead, gaining ground as usual. She swooped into a glade of trees and small boulders. I ran to catch up, unsure which direction she had gone. Separated from her, I hurried toward the convention halls that towered sternly overhead like soldiers.

Bumping into a scrawny young guy who seemed to be attempting to grow a beard, I mumbled an apology under my breath. "Hey," he said, "wanna fight"? He looked as though he weighed 90 pounds and I was not afraid.

"Fight you, what for"?

"Come on, old man," he said. "Let's take it outside."

"We are outside. And anyway, fighting never solved anything."

"Come on, come on," he muttered, lifting his bedraggled limbs.

"You are on a harmful life path," I said. "But there's still time to change."

"It's too late for me."

"No, it's not. Find something you love, something that helps other living beings. Follow it with passion."

"They all say that, but it's not true. It never works."

"It might not," I said. "But it might. Look at me. I followed my love of words and now I have a part time job teaching English, where I'm underappreciated and ineffective. I'm underpaid, but I'm not on the street starving."

"Thank you, sir," said the bedraggled youth. "No one ever cared enough about me to admit the truth."

I hurried on, glad that I had fooled him, afraid that he would realize what a hypocrite I am.

And You May Find Yourself . . . .

    I had gone back to college to attain an additional degree, as happens so often in dreams. Or was I returning to finish the first degree that I had never quite achieved? I was living in a suite with many roommates, lonely and away from my wife. The roommates were polite enough, but distant, and I disliked having to share my bed with a male. Some of our accidental household had gathered for a kind of meal, perhaps a tea with small, dry cakes, and they spoke softly, ignoring me. Why had I chosen to come here, instead of remaining with my wife where I was happy? Now it was too late and I felt I could never leave.

    I awoke and entered our huge living room, with gleaming white furniture and sun streaming in. My wife threw her arms around me, rained kisses upon me. "My darling, my darling," she said. "It's so good, ja." I noticed she spoke with a slight German accent, which was strange since my wife is from Boston. I realized this was not my wife, but a lovely, warm woman. Perhaps she is my wife now?

Portrait of the Artist

She was an artist. She excelled at the art of falling apart. Or rather, her work did. Over the years, she sent us various pillows, paintings, and sculptures, that slowly or quickly unraveled, or even shattered. Once, we received a beautiful pillow with a photo of Marianne and me surrounded by birds, sun, clouds and sky, lovely bits of riff raff stitched hither and about. We displayed it on our couch, knowing it wouldn't last. Piece by piece, it has come undone. Like a Tibetan sand painting destined to blow away in fierce winds, or a snow man with rocks for eyes, or a glittering ice sculpture that soon melts, the pillow was, is, will be ephemeral. Earlier, a bright collage, an abstract patchwork blazing with color, that the artist sent us fell to the floor and the glass covering shattered. It remains in storage, awaiting a new frame that we may never obtain. In the kitchen we had hung a tiny sculpture of a naked person, not quite man or woman or perhaps both, but it fell to the floor and shattered. This is not a metaphor about transgender or binary identity, but simply a testimony to our carelessness, or to the ravages of time, or to bad luck. This particular incident is no fault of the artist. Or perhaps it is; perhaps her works are imbued with self-destruction, an artistic statement emanating from her personality, or maybe from the vast spiritual realm, cast through her unwitting body, her consciousness, her artistic hands. Perhaps she means her works to last forever, but they die quicker than fruit flies.

Now our cat sits proudly upon the pillow's tattered remnants, perched upright like a living statue. Rumor has it that, when the masks the artist had sewed for the coronavirus outbreak fell apart, she finally learned to stitch properly. She is working hard to create something that lasts, a futile endeavor. The most profound artistic statement is the brevity of creation.

A Rambling Dream

My wife and I were in an enormous hotel room, rather like the inside of the Taj Mahal, our luggage, clothing, and toilet articles strewn about. We had evidently settled in for a long time. It was vast, but dark and gloomy.

I was on a beach throwing a frisbee with a bearded gentleman. We actually had a pile of frisbees and stepped away for hot dogs, which was strange since I do not eat meat. When we returned, a hipster was jumping on our frisbees as if to destroy them. Like the gentleman, the hipster had a beard. We went up to the hipster and he ran away, but we did not want to provoke a fight so we just let him go.

I told the bearded gentleman that I suddenly remembered my wife and I had to leave the hotel that day. She might already be gone. Unfortunately, I didn't remember the name of the hotel or know where it was located. I've always had this problem with memory and plan to do better in the future by writing down locations and phone numbers, but somehow never do. But next time, I vowed, I would—that is, if I ever found my hotel room and escaped this strange country. I also realized that I had left my cell phone back at the hotel. But even with the phone, I doubtless would have been unable to contact my wife as she keeps her phone off so that I will not disturb her. She often disappears for hours or even days with no explanation of where she could possibly be. Once she was gone for a whole century, but that was in another life.

Fire!

I was in the army. I had resisted joining, but there were no jobs and I needed to feed my family. Protests had erupted across the country to oust our glorious leader and my unit had been sent to put them down. In the middle of our radiant town square, protestors had erected a statue of a shining golden woman, breasts bared, arm raised, and banner aloft, a goddess leading her people to democracy. Whenever we approached, the protestors pelted us with eggs, stones, and garbage. We had thrice doused them with a vicious rain of pepper spray and tear gas, but they endured.
I feared the order to shoot. I imagined my rifle bursting with noise, smoke, and recoil, a bullet penetrating the vigorous young flesh of a protestor, snuffing out youth and dreams. But if I ignored the order, I would be imprisoned, perhaps executed for treason. The slaughter of the protestors would happen in any case. And who would feed my family then?

The order arrived and we marched forward. A smirking, black-haired young man with a rat face hurled a stone that smacked square on my left shoulder. It stung like hellfire and yet I was strangely numb. In harmony with my unit, I raised my rifle and aimed at the defiant mob.

Alone, Again!

I was alone, living in a dark basement apartment with a tiny kitchen in which I grilled cheap, greasy hamburger to sustain myself. A cockroach stuttered across the floor, but I was too tired to chase it. I wondered how I had spent so much of my life alone. Many years ago I had kissed a woman but now no one would have me. What had gone wrong with my life? Was I that unattractive? Did my rather squeaky voice wheedle and annoy? I thought I was kind to people, saying "please" and "thank you" to waitresses multiple times, for instance. Perhaps they found me obsequious, disgusting? Perhaps the secret to success was to be nasty? I awoke to the mewling of the cats begging to be fed, my wife beside me, as her warm hand touched my arm. Sunlight streamed through a crack in the shutters.

A Beast!

I stare at the trash can in the distance and a beast emerges. No, that's just a trick of the light glinting from the sun. But what if as I grow closer, an actual beast emerges? It could happen, as I believe I'm in the midst of a dream, and anything can happen in a dream. Beasts could pop up from the surrounding mist, a building in the distance could sprout legs and gallop toward me, eager to crush. At least, it could if I'm dreaming, but I don't believe I am.

Games Ain't What They Used to Be

I was in a house at the edge of a suburb at the edge of the city where I had come to play board games. Games had been getting more and more complicated lately. In front of me was a table with sparkling pieces of various shapes and colors and a large board with intricate flow charts and mathematical tables. Indeed, the game was so vast that it seemed to have no end, spilling off the table and beyond the horizon. The guy leading the game was guiding us through a huge manual, *The Book of All Wisdom and All Folly.* I had come late, and it was my turn, but I was having trouble wrapping my head around how to play, what the objective was, or which pieces were mine.

I looked up and noticed that all the players were gone. Dusk was streaming through the windows of the airless house. They had taken a break, or given up on me, and fled somewhere, perhaps to a bar. It was late, late on a dark dark winter's night and I realized that I had better catch the last bus. But I didn't have a schedule and didn't even know where the bus stop was. I remembered it was down a long block, and then I would have to turn somewhere, I couldn't remember whether right or left, and then there was some other strange movement kitty-corner, over a railing and down a small hill.

I opened *The Book of All Wisdom and All Folly,* hoping desperately it would guide me home.

Reincatnation

In the far future, Callie had returned to us in the form of a small tabby cat. "Didn't you do better in the reincarnation game?" I asked. "You were always good to us."

"Maybe she's being punished for being cruel to Thelma," said Marianne.

"Isn't that what cats do? Besides, she had reason to be jealous."

We were old and wizened. It wasn't clear how long we would be able to keep taking care of the cats.

There were actually three of them, as the original Callie and Thelma remained with us. Somehow, Callie had reincarnated before her death—after all, time is something of an illusion—and the two Callies rubbed against each other and purred. The scrawny ancient Callie was even smaller than the frisky, young tabby Callie. From the nearby couch, Thelma looked on aloof, like Buddha.

What Success Looks Like

At a conference, I ran into Tanya, a gorgeous woman who shimmered with life, a talented poet whose voice was the sound of diamonds glittering, yet a horrible person who had been a housemate my last year in graduate school. Her blonde boyfriend, a musician who looked like Adonis, had been so devoted to her he snuck into her bed when she wasn't around. "The poor sucker," I thought a few years later. "I wonder whatever became of him." Tanya was one of the stars at the convention, reading from her volume "How I Became Wonderful, Shiny Me," that had sold a million copies. Despite her success, I strode over to tell her what I really thought of her, but as I approached I became dumbstruck and stood there like an anxious puppy desperate to please its master. She flickered a faint smile, but I could hear her thoughts reverberating like feedback from a tacky guitar solo: "You loser. I knew you'd never amount to anything."

Destination: Nowhere

      I was riding my bicycle frantically, skimming over the surface of the orange ocean. Insecticides had rusted the vast water as far as the I could sea, making of it a viscous solution that sloshed beneath me soaking my boots, my socks, my quaking flesh. I was peddling like a starving gerbil on a vast wheel, food dangling just ahead, rushing to save the planet. Aliens had sabotaged the ocean, were corroding the air, the skies. Circling gulls squawked cruelly above. They, too, were starving, searching frantically for food, for land. I had no brakes, my gear shift was stuck, I could go only fast and faster, didn't know my destination or why I was peddling so frantically.

Well, I Dreamed . . .

The silver spaceship soared into the yellow haze of sun carrying all the world's billionaires. They were self-deporting, leaving this wretched ball as it writhes in its greed-induced sickness, to build a new life on Mars, or perhaps to perish in the blankness of space, or to suffer radiation, sickness, and suffering, or to starve slowly on the Martian surface or choke for lack of oxygen.

Your Birth Is Your Fate

In my dream, I was born an orthodox Jew, one of those funny little hats permanently attached to my head, a mutation unprecedented in science. I was deathly allergic to pork and shellfish. This was strange since my parents are in no way religious. I grew up a militant atheist, railing against the idea of G-d and the unfairness of the universe. Mostly people just ignored me.

Now, with anti-Semitism swelling across the globe, I find myself under fire. People rush away from me, afraid that I carry some virulent disease, though I could assure them that genetic mutations are not catching. True, if I had children with these racist strangers, G-d knows what the offspring would be. Perhaps they would have Yarmulkas attached to their heads even larger and more prominent than mine, perhaps they would be all Yarmulka, their humanness overtaken utterly, reduced to a symbol of Otherness. In any case, I don't want to breed with people on the street, just have them behave decently toward me.

Meanwhile, the anti-Semites grow bolder. From a distance, the other day, a woman shouted out, "too bad Hitler didn't kill all of you." And just this morning, a man sprang at me, slapped my face, then backed away as if I were some diseased thing. It's only a matter of time before the knife or the gun that ends this bizarre experiment that is my life.

f She Floats, She's a Witch

I stared into the empty coffee cup. It was perfect in every
way—the circle of the lid, the white and shadows of the interior,
ven the intricate grains of the stains it had picked up. Somehow, I
new I was dreaming, how could the cup not be real? I decided the
rue test would be to drop the cup and use my powers of levitation.
f it floated, I was dreaming. I released the handle.

Way Down Under

I was on a bus to visit my sister, who lived far down South among the cotton trees and sharecroppers. She had developed a massive southern accent and I often needed captions to understand her. The bus weaved through the red earth under an ominous gray sky. I gazed out expecting to see the sting of the whip and fresh blood on exposed backs, but then I remembered that slavery had ended at least a decade ago.

Suddenly, I realized that my sister had recently moved to a smaller town in a swamp in the deeper south, so deep it almost fell off the edge of the world, so deep I wondered whether it was close enough to Antarctica to actually be cold. Perhaps the swamp water would freeze, leaving perfect fossils of frogs and penguins to be found by some newly intelligent species hundreds of millions of years away, after humanity has long vanished. Rain sputtered outside as the sky blackened and, with a bolt of electricity edging through my spine, I pondered asking the bus driver to turn back. O perhaps there was a transfer to get to my sister, but how would I find out when or where and lightening was flashing in the distance as our ancient bus stalled and roared, stalled and roared.

I Gaze Down on the City, Gape up at the Stars

Like King Kong (although punier and weaker), I was atop a massive tower, gazing out over a vast, shining city with golden mosques and church spires glinting in the sun. It was getting hot and I felt an anxious need to be somewhere, doing something productive, so I started to head down the spiral staircase. But crowds of tourists were ascending, blocking the stairway so I backed up to let them pass. I backed and backed till I realized that I had somehow missed another stairway even higher. I realized if I tried to ascend backward I would probably trip and fall into the infinite sky, so I'd better turn and head upward. When the restless mob of vaguely Asian tourists wielding shiny cameras passed, I could then head down.

I ran and ran, upward upward, outpacing the clamoring crowd, panting and dripping in the midday heat, taking occasional gulps from a leather water bottle. I ran till the city was a tiny dot I glanced at occasionally below, ran to where day meets night, out among the stars, where the cool breath of darkness, interrupted by brilliant patches of star, soothed my soul. Above, the glowing orb of the moon smiled on me, beckoning. I took a huge breath and leapt.

Spiral

I was delighted when I discovered a bicycling route that was downhill all the way, from when I left home, north through the tunnel under a nearby river, east where I sped down a steep hill, south through a section of town strewn with parking lots and light industry, then down a gentle slope, west, through a wooded area atwitter with birds, after which I would return to our cozy, yellow home. This route would make my thrice weekly exercise fun and easy!

I was perturbed when my wife pointed out that to bicycle only downhill and return to the same spot broke basic laws of physics. The route must exist in some bizarre rupture in the spatial continuum, perhaps even in the space-time continuum, and I likely wasn't returning to quite the same version of reality. Indeed, I had noticed that the house seemed slightly different each time, sometimes with a porch, sometimes a different shade of yellow, sometimes with a sprucer lawn, sometimes with an extra little room tucked away in the back. And my wife herself varied: her hair was now slightly blonde, she seemed taller, more shapely, with a more razor-sharp mind than she had in the past. Before she spoke up, I had been willing to overlook these differences since, after all, who doesn't like an easy way to exercise?

All this presented a conundrum. If I was indeed returning to altered realities, does this mean that another version of me had been previously occupying that reality and was now in some slightly alternative world? Does this mean that I had abandoned other versions of my wife, bike-ride by bike-ride? Does this mean that versions of my wife in other realities were left to live out their lives alone?

To be a moral person, there was only one remedy. I would have to reverse my route, taking an arduous uphill ride three times a week. But was I in shape for it? What if my legs, or even my heart, gave out? Did I have the mental energy for such an endeavor? And what if the version of me in the previous world—who must have been biking in from an even earlier world--decided he was too lazy for this route? How would I handle it if I ran into another me?

60

The next day, I began my downhill route again, putting off for another time the terrible climb uphill.

A Game of Chance

The crone always sat twisted on the gates to the city and, as I passed every day, invited me to a game of backgammon for a meager wager. Assuming my best yoga pose, I would join her on the powdery dirt. The dice clambered, pieces engaged back and forth, I would be down to one piece perched on the last space before victory, and she would roll double sixes once again. I wondered how to calculate the mathematical odds of this happening, day after day, year after year, millennium after millennium—they must be a trillion to one. Still, I felt I could peer into her depths and she was an honest soul. Perhaps the forces that rule the universe allowed her to win, to keep her meager life going. One day, just as she was about to beat me again, I glanced at her and she was a shining maiden in a golden dress, her face fair as the day, her breath sweet as honey. I figured the universe was repaying me for my goodness and bent over to kiss her. But as her tongue lunged into my throat she transformed again into the crone and her foul breath wreaked into me. Her tongue plunged down, down, down, strangling, into my esophagus.

Dinners with My Wife

My wife and I sat down at the table. I admired her shining
blonde hair, her icy blue eyes, gazing at me. Was that love I saw?
Or a predator stalking its victim?

*

My wife and I sat down to dine. I admired her fuzzy hair
black as black, her shining brown skin. She smiled, gazed at me in
adoration. But was she adoring me or just the fact that she had
nagged a white man, a kind of trophy? Or was it disgust at the
hundreds of years of slavery, rape, segregation, exploitation, my
kind had brought upon her people? It wasn't me who did it, I
swear, I'm just an individual, innocent of history, trying to live my
one, insignificant life as best I can.

*

My wives and I sat down for a feast. My wives ringed the
table, 80 virgins, eyes shining from behind their snow-white
burkas. I wasn't having much fun at night, what with their
insistence on continued virginity, but still it gave me a thrill to
have them ringed around, seemingly at my beck and call, though
that, of course, was an illusion. Perhaps others saw through it, too?

Beyond Siberia

I was in a jam-packed bus, sweating profusely in the winter heat. Struggling not to disturb the grossly fat man snoozing beside me, whose elbow protruded into my side, whose widespread legs squeezed me on the outer seat, constantly on the verge of tumbling into the aisle, I squirmed out of my vast fur coat bit by excruciating bit. Triumphantly, I arose and tucked the coat into the rack above, inadvertently elbowing the other obese man who spilled out of the seat across the aisle and glared at me. Back in my seat, I realized I had been wearing only underwear, riddled with holes, beneath the coat. Freezing air blasted and I shivered violently as the sweat that drenched me turned to ice. I arose to retrieve the coat from above, pulled the massive, furry thing, roll after roll, swaddled myself in its thickness. Back in my seat, heat poured from the bus's ventilation, and the cycle began again. I remembered that this retrieving and replacing of the coat had been going on for at least a thousand miles, as I gazed at the blinding icy landscape. Perhaps I should just remain sitting here until I froze to death or melted into a puddle of water? What was this life, anyway? Why was I traveling in the far north? Or was it south? Where had I come from, what was my destination? Who, even, was I? And in the larger scheme of things, or even the smaller scheme, did it really matter to anyone but me? Did I even matter to myself? But then I remembered that I had a wife and she, at least, cared for me even though nobody else on the planet did. I would journey on in the hope that I would one day see her again.

Another Wall Story

Crowds gaped at me from all directions, shouting, gaping, jeering, whooping. I was in an arena at some kind of contest, wearing only a snowy white thong.

It was a tennis match. From the inept amateur I had been a year earlier, I had, through force of will that emanated from some unknown place almost outside myself, through diving for loose balls, scrambling for seemingly impossible shots, and thinking two or three steps ahead of my opponents, clawed my way into the championship match of a grand slam event. It was taking place in a faraway country under a yellow sky. I glanced across the gleaming green court at my opponent—a concrete wall, of no particular color, that rose to the heavens. I could not hit over it. It stretched beyond the horizon in every direction, so there was no way to hit a clever spinning shot around it. Nor could I, with my feeble arms so unlike those of a tennis champion, use sheer power to drill my way through the wall. I had lost before I began.

The wall, of course, is a metaphor, but of what, you ask? Of the great divide between east and west? Of an authoritarian surveillance state? Of interfering teachers and parents who choke young people's efforts to develop any kind of individuality? Of cruelty to immigrants? Of all these things and more?

The wall is no metaphor. That's the cop out, the easy way. The wall is real, a literal concrete image of the kind so many teachers tell us to write about. The wall exists not in story but in reality. I am down 1 game to 0 and it is the wall's turn to serve, but it cannot. However, there is no umpire to call the game and it lingers on. It's been lingering for eons, perhaps since before the game of tennis was even invented.

I Get in Trouble Once Again

I have wandering eyes. They will, from time to time, pop out of their sockets, sprout little wings, and fly away to stare at some hapless victim, usually a woman but sometimes a man. Once they've picked their victim, I cannot call them back. Like Coyote's penis in native American myth, which detaches itself and roves about on rowdy adventures, my eyes take on a mind of their own. I may be worse off than Coyote, since he is only desexed for a time, whereas I am blind. And the eyes continue to pick on the same victim time and again. "Is that your detached eyes that have been staring at me?" one tall, tattooed ruffian of a woman demanded of me recently and I could only shrug my shoulders hopelessly as her switchblade plunged at my exposed belly. Or perhaps I was only imagining it, as I was blind.

Atonement

I congratulated myself for having an entire day when I didn't eat a single animal. It happens more and more often. I am a flexitarian, verging on vegetarianism, but I always lapse. In my lengthening life, I've already eaten menageries, zoos full. Squawking chickens; cows beautiful and bountiful in black and white, huge and mooing and flowing with rivers of milk; huge brown pigs wriggling in the mud, oinking merrily; schools of fish, silvery and darting; hordes of shrimp scuttering through the ocean depths. This bountiful feast has passed through my mouth, down my throat, through my stomach and guts, and returned in far less beautiful form than it started, back to the mud and the sewers and the primeval waters.

I would apologize, but what good would it do? No more good than apologizing for slavery or the genocide of Native Americans. I didn't do any of those horrible things, though in a way I'm a beneficiary.

I would bless the animals, thank them for the nourishment they gave me, thank their divine spirits, as some Native Americans do. But what right do I have to apologize and bless, I who do not even have the guts, the balls, the spirit, to hunt and fish them myself? I prefer to have them killed for me, packaged on distant assembly lines by anonymous laborers working vast swathes of hours to barely survive. Indeed, the great majority of the animals I've eaten were neither free ranging, nor living on idyllic farms, but jammed into crates, existing only as commodities, not as living, breathing, sentient beings. Should I say a prayer to them?

The Word

The word was out—final, definitive proof of the existence of God had been discovered in a part of the Middle East so distant it was on the other side of the planet, and then another thousand miles beyond. Dressed as a Knight of the Round Table, I set out to find the final proof so that humanity, knowing there was ultimate purpose, would not suffer any more, or at least would suffer a bit less.

I set out on a twisty, torturous, dusty road across vast fields through thick woods, over rolling hills. For a small portion of the journey, I was actually atop a horse (although a beaten-down old nag), but most of the time I merely banged two coconuts together. travelled high atop craggy mountains, through deep tunnels in primordial darkness beset with dripping, fording mighty rivers, stowing aboard various barges and one dragon ship to cross vast oceans and little streams. Along the way, I consulted with a wise mystic atop a mountain peak, several viziers, and one particularly brilliant court jester. I fought three ruffians, two of whom were assaulting maidens and one who was just a loud-mouthed imbecile (Alas, I won only one of those three battles.) I even slayed a dragon, albeit a particularly small, innocuous one who wasn't doing any harm but had scared some of the locals (I still feel guilty about that one). Finally, after a thousand days, a thousand nights, and 3.1416 seconds, I arrived at a golden shrine. Glorious hymns rose up in the morning sun as I opened an ornate vessel atop the shrine and pulled out a faded yellow parchment. On it were three statements, a syllogism of sorts:
—this paper is the word of God.
—The word of God is infallible.
—God exists because this paper says so.

Salvador Dali Races On

Racing my bike so fast I broke the sound barrier, I didn't notice the shard of glass glistening on the bridge. I skidded, spun, barely held on. The flat tire was so extreme, the whole wheel melted, metal rim, spokes, and all, and dripped, leaking away into crack in the pavement.

My Wife Tells Me of Her Dream

My wife was ending a European vacation, taking a train back to Maryland, but not sure whether to take the eastbound or westbound. She hopped on the first train that came by, thinking she could ask the conductor and change at the next stop, if necessary. "You're going all the way to Maryland?" he said, astonished, in a thick European accent. "I'm not sure what train to take—I'll have to ask Hans. But he's disappeared, I'll let you know as soon as I see him. But it's 31 minutes till the next stop—I'm sure he'll show up by then."

Thirty-one minutes! So long just for one stop! It was nothing like the DC Metro system. Europe must sprawl over half the globe. And she would be stuck in some cold, isolated city in the far north waiting to get back, safe, safe, to our cozy Maryland home.

"That's exactly like one of my dreams," I told my wife.

ne Day in an Orchard

At my feet were piles of apples, green streaked with red, a ild red, a ruby red, a blood red struggling to shine through. I lanced up and realized I was in an orchard, trees shimmering with pples.

I sensed that one of the apples was THE one, the apple of n and knowledge. Eating it would complete the circle begun by ve which had signaled the start of human history. Eating it would ring about the apocalypse. I must not eat it. Yet I must, I felt ompelled, it was time. Could it possibly be that I, who felt myself mong the least significant people on the planet, as insignificant as ne untouchables in India, the slaves that inhabit the hidden places round the globe, the child labor in the poorest of countries, the irls sold as sex slaves, the prisoners who stuff the jails with earning in the United States even today, would be the catalyst for ne end of time?

I picked up the first apple, took an enormous bite. It was lightly bitter but mostly bland, not at all juicy. It choked me, but I agged it down. Apples had never been my favorite fruit, and these vere among the dullest of apples. If I only forced myself to smaller ites, eating them would not be unpleasant, just boring, and there vas a whole orchardful. I could spend the rest of my life here, eat pple after apple, and still never find the apple of the knowledge of ood and evil.

I took a second bite.

Transmigration

One day Thelma came to us in the form of a dog, a smallish mutt of indeterminate color, although perhaps still tabby. She bounded around as we patted her, then leapt up and curled on the couch to sleep.

Most days, Thelma did choose to remain a cat, but one day she scurried about as a worried-looking rabbit. Another time, she was a sloth, hanging from our ceiling fan, and once a lion cub, which was scary—how would we handle her if she grew to a full thousand-pound beast? When Thelma took the form of a deer, she bounded about the house in a panic, knocking over our kitchen table and breaking several dishes. "Don't ever do that again," I told her sternly, once she had returned to cat form.

"What if she appears as a mythological creature?" Marianne asked with a worried look. "If she starts breathing fire, she could really do some damage. Maybe we need better insurance?"

"Don't be ridiculous," I said. "Dragons and whatnot don't even exist. You've got to start living in the real world."

I was more worried that Thelma would take the form of an insect and we would accidentally step on her. Then that would be the end of our wonderful cat!

An Accident

I was in the passenger seat on a trek across Australia, or some other distant continent, where wildness still reigns, at least in spots. My driver was Fatima Karma, who had earlier edited my work and gone on to better things at a legendary think tank. I had written her intermittently asking about freelance work, but hadn't received a reply. Now here she was, chauffeuring me into the heart of the unknown. In the distance, across sandy plains punctuated by tufts of grass and occasional palm trees, wildebeests galloped in thick masses while vultures swooped overhead. As we drove, livestock thickened in front of us, gnarly cow-like things with unkempt hair like something out of Dr. Seuss (or is Dr. Seuss like something out of the natural world?). We stopped briefly, surrounded by braying beasts, but they soon dissipated like smoke from a campfire in a high wind, and we drove on down the open road. Fatima complained that I should share the driving, but I explained that my license had been taken away. She retreated to a back seat, where she could continue driving slouched sideways, legs up. Fortunately, there was an extra steering wheel and gas pedal in the back (but were there brakes?) but I worried that she would be unable to fully guide the vehicle. In the distance, the silhouettes of great beasts moved gradually closer. Massive golden rams, powerful mountainous beasts, Buddhas of the plains. Perhaps they would save our dying planet, restore nature's grand order? A great snore emanated from Fatima's wide open mouth as our jeep skidded off the open road.

The End, Delayed

I had thought about staging my own funeral, sneaking in to view it, like Huck Finn. It would be the only time people would gather to praise me. Long lost family members would reappear, proclaim their love for me, though they never bothered to do so while I was alive.

One thing keeps me from staging my own death, though. What if no one bothered to show up at the funeral and I just crouched behind a scraggly stand of bushes, gazing at emptiness?

Dreamin' and Schemin' until I'm Screamin'

I was a business mogul, fantastically successful, rich beyond my dreams (which had never particularly involved money)! My scheme had been to open a series of adventure camps where people ran around in enormous, clear spheres made of space-age plexiglass, like giant hamsters. Years ago, I had visited a house where a hamster ran around in its hamster-ball among the cats who batted at it, sent it spinning to every corner. The hamster remained unharmed and seemed to enjoy the experience. My inspiration had been to do the same for people, and in my adventure parks lions, tigers, bears, oh my even elephants, kicked and spun people in their plexiglass balls (participants had to sign a release form absolving my company of liability for injuries). One time I went in person to the keystone adventure park, in Africa, where Safari animals thundered, made slightly mad by hunger, steroids, and amphetamine injections. I had strayed from the plush central building to an unknown corner of the park and dusk was approaching. An enormous elephant gave me the boot, sent me spinning straight into a pack of lions that galloped madly, yellow eyes glowing like moons. I was stunned, unable to control my plexiglass sphere, as they batted at me. Would I be forced to stay the night, soiling myself and being rescued in the morning in a humiliating fashion? The lions soon lost interest, but an enormous baboon had climbed atop my sphere. Could a baboon possibly grow that large? Was it the steroids? Perhaps he had been fed too many since infancy, or even in the womb? Somehow, he had gotten hold of a massive spike and as he hammered repeatedly the plexiglass cracked.

Life Gets Harder

A vagrant had broken into our kitchen, and was seen scuttling behind the refrigerator and lurking in the dark corners. Most likely, she was diseased. We would have to eradicate her. We'd already tried the most humane way, a catch-and-release trap, but it hadn't fooled her and she remained, a scampering shape at dusk, gathering up scraps of our food. We knew what had to come next—a snap-trap, or poison. The snap-trap was cruel, but Marianne was worried that poison would harm our wonderful cat, Thelma.

On television, the news spoke of growing throngs of hungry humans, desperate and only too willing to break into good people's houses.

In my mind, I envisioned the vagrant's corpse collapsed on the floor, thin body and broken twigs of limbs, a twisted heap, a remnant. I imagined myself picking up the broken body, grasping it awkwardly beneath the armpits and dragging it out to the curb to be removed on garbage day.

My Wife Gets in the Way

I go to my computer but can't use it because my wife is here printing out assignments for her class. So I head to the bathroom to floss, but somehow my wife has beat me to it and the closed door glares at me forbiddingly. So I get ready to do my exercises, but my wife is tromping across the floor carrying laundry.

In every room is the cat, curled up asleep, or yowling for attention, but I am too busy to spend time with her, trying to get ready for my day. Soon I will leave. Another morning wasted.

My wife seems annoyed. "You've been getting in the way all morning," she tells me.

Yet Another Meaningless Journey

As I step onto the bus, I see one section is empty and another packed with minority groups in a variety of shapes and colors, from light olive to chocolate brown. I notice a puddle of icy brown water—a spilled coke, perhaps?—in the only empty seat in the minority section. But if I were to sit in the majority section, what would they think of me? Perhaps a tall, dark man with preternaturally curly pitch-black hair would come over and stab me in my exposed gut. Unlikely, but all of their eyes staring at me would be humiliating. Or perhaps they would look away, embarrassed themselves. However, I had never felt myself a member of that tiny number of blonde, blue-eyed barbarians that constitute the majority of our society. I strode confidently over to the minority section, hesitated, then sat timidly down, soaking my pants in the ugly brown fluid, prepared to ride for hours, days, a lifetime if needed pretending to be comfortable.

A small man tapped me lightly from behind. "You don't need to sit in that mess," he said. "There are plenty of empty seats on this bus."

Legacy

I still feel bad, at times, about my grandparents. After all, they played an enormous part in raising me, grandmother bustling about the house, singing snatches of old folk songs, preparing food, grandpa taking me out to the nearby hills, hiking with me, teaching me to tend the sheep in our pasture. It was he who was sent away first, on a "special vacation." I was too young to connect this with the delicious meat, somewhat like chicken somewhat like lamb, that appeared in the next days and weeks, alongside potatoes, in stews, in soups. But when they sent grandma away and the same thing happened, the realization came to me in the middle of a tasty cutlet.

Sure, I was upset, but I've grown wiser since. After all, they were only continuing the nourishment they'd been giving me all along, donating something of themselves to make me happy and healthy. I've heard that in other countries and places they would consider the practice barbaric. But what's the alternative, to have them grow infirm, their bodies breaking down, their vision and hearing fading, as they soil themselves and their minds slowly disintegrate? That would be the true barbarism!

The Great Cycle of Life

There's an old man in my living room, moaning and groaning just like my dad used to do, and I think it's me!

Horror Movie!

Covid 19 had mutated and was turning people into zombies. I was out for a stroll in a large park, streaming with daylight, with birds. In the distance, a slovenly woman in a large potato sack of a dress with stringy black hair stumbled toward me. The lovely music of the birds twittered around, the sunlight beckoned, the trees drew me in with their shapely green leaves. I planned to give the woman a wide berth, but as I approached she moved awkwardly to one side, then the other, as I attempted to pass. Out of her fat fleshy face, dull brown eyes gazed vacuously, and I noticed flecks of foam on her lips. I felt spritely enough to evade her yet somehow stood paralyzed.

Fortunately, the zombie effect would only last for a couple of weeks. It could be interesting—my life as a zombie. Perhaps I would write a memoir. Zombies are still in fashion, as far as I can remember. I would be rich, a famous author! Though perhaps the hundreds of millions of people infected around the world would only want to forget their experience as zombies.

Everything Is Everything

If they have an Everything Bagel, can a Theory of Everything be far behind?

But wait, isn't a Theory of Everything necessary before on can create an Everything Bagel?

What's in the hole of a bagel? Nothing? What's the opposite of nothing? Everything! So doesn't the surrounding bagel have to be everything?

Perhaps something is the opposite of nothing. But then everything is not the opposite of something which means that everything does not exist. On the other hand, nothing is something that doesn't exist so if everything does not exist that makes it the equivalent of nothing. So, something and everything would be opposites. But something is the subset of everything.

Conversation at a Party

"Death, what's that? People talk about it in mysterious tones, but the truth is, nobody's ever explained to me what it is."

We all have our strange ideas, holes in our knowledge. On the radio, I had heard of a woman who didn't know that unicorns were fantasy creatures and was humiliated when she found out. But what adult doesn't know about death? Yet here was this young woman with a round face and innocent eyes asking me to explain death. Still, I guess everyone has to learn some time, and it seemed my fate to explain.

It was a simple party, not well attended but pleasant, with soft flute music in the background. I began.

What did I tell her? That death is when you sleep forever, dreaming of realms of beauty and harmony, but that these realms are real and our world the illusion? That death is a particularly nasty disease, with fevers, boils, paralysis, vomiting, constricted breathing, heart palpitations, but that you recover and all is as it was? That, just as you are born from the womb of a woman, when you grow old and shrink enough, you return to the womb (albeit of a new, much younger woman)? That death was the cessation of all consciousness forever?

I don't remember when I, myself learned about death, or sex for that matter. My parents told me very young. Or perhaps I just always knew.

After I explained death, the young woman gazed at me with wicked eyes. Had they once been soft and brown? They appeared green and hard, boring through my very soul. Or had they always been that way, luring me into losing my innocence?

Contact

Likely the strongest counter to the theory of intelligent life throughout the universe is the question, where are they? Why haven't they tried to contact us?

In a dream, great civilizations scattered throughout this universe beamed signals to Earth to announce their presence. The space between stars is so huge that it took millennia for the signals to reach us. Meanwhile, climate change wracked the Earth, great cities flooded, whole species died like flies (including species of flies). Human refugees flocked over borders to be met by incarceration, gunfire, and poison gas. Conflict intensified, ending in nuclear exchange. The day after we humans destroyed ourselves, news arrived from numerous corners, nooks, and crannies of the universe that we are not the only intelligent life.

A Great Social Issue Remains Unsolved

I was a woman, waking from anesthetized dreams after an abortion. The table was small and cold, but the nurse held my hand warmly. The vivid faces of the abortion protesters flickered in my memory, zombies with fangs and vivid gashes, victims of the plague. I wept for the death of my daughter, but how could I give birth alone and friendless amid a plague?

Afterward, I stumbled out into the cold rays of the setting sun terrified of facing the jagged line of zombies once again. Perhaps this time one would bite, puncture my skin, turn me into a zombie? But the streets were deserted. I stumbled past tall, empty, cold buildings realizing I had exited the wrong way. Where was my car? How would I get myself home?

Safari

Rumors swirled that a lion had escaped, was bounding about Rockville. It was spotted at Maryvale Park, at the Woodside Deli, atop the clock tower on the Colony Bank building. The police and animal control could never pin it down and, even with ubiquitous cell phones, no one had quite been able to snap a photo. My wife was driving us home, which was fortunate as I had given up my license years ago and she had never learned to drive. Yet suddenly, she had mastered the skill and now we wafted along in a tiny red Corvette as though atop some magic carpet. Suddenly, I spotted it atop the gas station on the street leading to our house. An enormous beast, crouched on great haunches, yellow with a shaggy mane, piercing us with its fierce green eyes, saliva dripping from its gaping mouth, fangs gleaming poised like white scimitars. Swiftly and skillfully, my wife backed away, executed a turn, and we zoomed off.

"We'll just take a different route," she said nonchalantly, driving with one hand on the wheel down a pleasant side street past brightly colored houses.

"Whew," I said, "that was close," not quite noticing the rhino ahead, poised to charge.

The Art of Naming

Once a woman loved her daughter so much, she yearned to give her a name that encompassed the world. She endowed the infant with name upon name, first names, middle names, a multiply hyphenated last name. Each name in her language had meaning: birds, beasts, plants, the earth, the sky, the divine spirit, the demi-gods, love, carnal satisfaction, joy, tears, death, rebirth, and more. When the woman had exhausted her language, she felt she still had not fully designated all of her love and began to invent new words, new names. She is doing this still. Perhaps, when she is finished, the world will end and the divine one will descend from a crack in the sky. Perhaps the divine one will be the woman's daughter, fully grown, ready to fill the world with love. Perhaps the daughter, swelling with anger at all the injustice in the world, as catalogued in her infinite names, will be an avenging devil strewing fire, plague, torture, and death. Most likely, she has already begun.

Side Entrance

Somehow, a small orange cat had gotten into the house. I recognized it as our neighbor's and shouted to her, asking how the cat had infiltrated. She explained that there was a side entrance exactly big enough for the cat. Just then, her enormous yellow Saint Bernard bounded over to the side entrance, perhaps to lick me, perhaps to bite. She grabbed it, though it appeared far too big to slip through. But who knows with animals? They find a way. Humans, too, and I realized I had better lock up that previously overlooked side door, though there were likely scores more, holes, gaps, secret entrances, through which thousands of infiltrators could slip.

The whole situation should not have been surprising. Our house is small, neat, and modest, although overflowing with papers, books, and electronic equipment in every cranny and beyond, spilling outdoors and flying over to our neighbors' yards on windy days. Inside the house, we keep finding small rooms—attics, basements, porches—that we hadn't realized were there, some dark and dusty, some overflowing with light from the heavens, bursts from stars in the darkest night. I rummaged through the ever-growing piles of junk to find an old lock with two silver keys—it's always nice to have a spare in case one is lost. Perfect for securing the newly discovered side entrance, which the entire neighborhood seems to have known about for eons.

What Goes 'Round Comes 'Round

There was a fight outside our house, two guys pummeling each other, one in a ripped orange shirt, the other in overalls with no shirt whatsoever, a flurry of fists, sweat spattering. "Should I call the police?" I asked my wife, but she was distracted, head bent over her laptop, grading papers. The larger dude, lean, well-muscled, sent an array of fists into the face of the smaller, who collapsed on the ground. Just as I was dialing 911, the smaller got up laughing. It was all a joke, a theater, as so many things are in life.

It was deadly serious, life and death, the grinning smaller figure abject, surrendering, humiliated. The bully always wins and there is no 911.

Life, Itself

Is Life a tale told by an idiot, a cereal, or a game?

In America, it's full of sound, fury, carbs, and sugar, with big winners and enormous losers.

Marianne Dreams of Her Life after Death

I gaze down from purgatory at my husband in Hell. If only he had accepted Jesus. I tried, I tried, Lord knows I tried. "Deep in my heart," he told me once, "I don't believe." Perhaps it was foolish to even attempt to convince him, as one cannot budge an unmoveable object. But what choice did I have?

My husband, the wry poet, the maniacal comedian who entertained me in the best years of my life, the tender cook and lover, the migraine victim who slept for hours and hours, the tortured young man with migraines given to bursts of anger, is strung upon a huge wooden cross, a tiny, contorted figure in the midst of Hell, surrounded by flames that lick, by demons that prick with innumerable spears, sending drops of blood sizzling into the hungry, angry flames. A radiant light shines from his forehead. Am I in purgatory—suspended in a heavy gray cloud just below the heavens, gazing down—for my transgressions, my anger, my sloth, my gluttony, my gossiping? Or am I trapped here only because I won't give up on my husband? Perhaps I'm as obstinate as he is? I'll never give up, but I'll never forgive his obstinacy. If he had only pretended to believe, perhaps that would be enough. Perhaps true belief would have followed pretense and we would be floating, joyous, in the upper heavens, now and forever, surrounded by radiant light, not pausing to glance at the torment below.

The Mouse Is a Chess Grandmaster

Had that mouse been in our house forever? I remembered her tormenting our cats, dancing past them. In fact, she appeared just before we inherited Callie from my mother. "Ha," I thought, "what horrid timing for the poor creature; our new cat will soon take care of her." It turned out Callie was pathetic as a mouser, swift and aggressive, yes, but clumsy, pouncing blindly, swiping at empty air, as the little rodent dashed past. Even when we got Thelma, a more thoughtful and methodical hunter, the clever mouse continued to win their chess games, darting from some unexpected corner, or scuttering out from under the stove or refrigerator, taking strange, unexpected turns in mid-flight that defied the laws of physics.

My wife thinks it was not one mouse, but many, some small and bright-eyed, others browner, fatter, furrier. And there were months and years when the mouse did not appear. But I know better. If it was not the same mouse physically, growing older, more filled out, slower but wiser over the years, it was the same mouse spiritually. My wife is too hung up over the physical world, linear thinking, natural laws, to realize that the very same being has been tormenting our poor cats over all these centuries. And now the mouse has appeared again, in the form of a cat, like a pawn that has advanced to the last row and been promoted to Queen. Now the mouse is the new Callie, small, energetic, calico yet darker, in tortoiseshell form. Instead of a filthy scourge that we fear will sicken us, she is now our best beloved. And now a new mouse—or is it the same old mouse?—has reemerged to torment her.

Build Worlds of Sand

I was a composer, writing poems with no rhyme, rhythm or reason. Stories with no beginning, middle, or end. Songs with no melody which I would sing in my high, scratchy voice as I improvised. I was composing the world, or trying to, but I lacked the skill to create even one human being, even one cockroach, one bacteria, one virus, each of which is ornate and beautiful without end. I was casting out words like a vast net, trying to capture something tangible, but spilling out on an empty universe. Was I creating meaning from emptiness, or perhaps spewing out emptiness into a universe filled with meaning? Houses and castles, fields and streams, birds and beasts, maidens and mad men, dreamers and thinkers and doers, composed entirely of words. Word after word without grammar, without syntax, without structure.

The Poet Edits the Manuscript

     I have a manuscript of poetry so wild, colorful, and vivid it encompasses an entire universe. But wait, there are flaws in the manuscript. I edit it down, word by word, line by line, image by image, poem by poem. I prune and remove each imperfection. Soon nothing is left but a blank document.
I begin again.

Acknowledgements:

The author gratefully acknowledges the following journals for publishing versions of these stories:

Alien Buddha – "Dreamin' and Schemin' Until I'm Screamin'."

Mad Swirl – "Life Advice."

The Raw Art Review – "Cattle Farm," "One Day in an Orchard," and "The Word."

Setu – "The Creation" and "Making a Spectacle of My Life."

Unlikely Stories – "Your Birth Is Your Fate."

Praise for the Fiction of Ethan Goffman

DREAMSCAPES by Ethan Goffman:

It is the exceptional poet who achieves the mastery of being able to come at us from multiple angles and never allow any of those perspectives to weaken under the weight of its equivalents. One consideration may take the lead - say, for example "gravity" - *Outlaws had captured me, stolen my gold, tied me to a stake, doused me with gasoline, and were ready to set me aflame* - followed almost immediately by "humor," sometimes bordering on unadulterated comedy, and whose function as "reliever" is flawless - *when who should swoop in to save me but the Lone Ranger and Tonto.*

Goffman is also capable, at the same time, of moving from the "deeply speculative" - *It is possible we're the only planet in the universe on which advanced life forms evolved. It is possible we're just one of billions of worlds teeming with life.* - to the "profoundly pragmatic" and self-effacing - *The only philosophy that makes any sense is utter uncertainty. Or perhaps I am being arrogant and foolish in making this pronouncement.*

And it all happens under one roof - *solemnity, wit, supposition,* practicality = and sometimes at breakneck speed.

You've all heard the term "page turner?" Never self-important, yet never self-diminishing, Ethan Goffman presents that "page turner" to us in **Dreamscapes**; he places it in our hands, and proclaims, *"Ready! Set! Go!"* But don't sit on your hands. You never know what's around the next page - *there are flaws in the manuscript. I edit it down, word by word, line by line, image by image, poem by poem. I prune and remove each imperfection. Soon nothing is left but a blank document.*

I begin again.

Dreamscapes is a wonderful and utterly compelling book.

John L. Stanizzi
Author of **Sundowning**, **POND**, *and nine other collections*

A descendant of Kafka lives among us and his name is Ethan Goffman."

Novelist Brian Morton, Recipient of the Guggenheim Foundation Fellowship, the Award in Literature from the American Academy of Arts and Letters, the Pushcart Prize and finalist for the PEN/Faulkner Award and the Kirkus Prize for Fiction

---

Ethan Goffman's *Dreamscapes* takes us on a surreal journey through worlds built of sand where "the only philosophy that makes any sense is utter uncertainty" and where the world is both utterly transformed" and simultaneously "the same." Goffman processes the events of our time through dream material that is sometimes satirical, sometimes provocative, but always engaging. These vignettes dream "the world into existence" and take us to the edge of the universe" where bicycle wheels melt, drip and leak away into a crack in the pavement," where art disintegrates, and where vision allows us to peer into our minds and histories. This collection provides thought-provoking escape from our current pandemic reality.

Claudine Nash, author of *Beginner's Guide to Loss in the Multiverse* and nominee for the Pulitzer, Pushcart, and Best of Net awards

Ethan Goffman's first volume of poetry *Words for Things Left Unsaid,* was published by Kelsay Books in March 2020. His poems and flash fiction have appeared in *Alien Buddha, Ariel Chart, BlazeVox, Bradlaugh's Finger, Bourgeon, EarthTalk, Literary Yard, The Loch Raven Review, Mad Swirl, Madness Muse, Piker Press, Ramingo's Blog, The Raw Art Review, Setu, Unlikely Stories, Verse Virtual* and elsewhere. Ethan is co-founder of It Takes a Community, a Montgomery College initiative bringing poetry to students and local residents. He is founder and producer of the *Poetry & Plane* podcast on EarthTalk.org. Ethan also writes on transportation issues for *Mobility Lab,* focusing on alternatives to automobile trips.

Made in the USA
Middletown, DE
14 December 2022

18391505R10064